PRETTY GOBLINS

ALSO BY BETH GRAHAM

The Drowning Girls and Comrades
(with Charlie Tomlinson and Daniela Vlaskalic)
The Gravitational Pull of Bernice Trimble

PRETTY GOBLINS

BETH GRAHAM

PLAYWRIGHTS CANADA PRESS
TORONTO

For professional or amateur production rights, please contact:
Ian Arnold at Catalyst TCM
15 Old Primrose Lane, Toronto, ON M5A 4T1
416-568-8673 | ian@catalysttcm.com

LIBRARY AND ARCHIVES CANADA CATALOGUING IN PUBLICATION
Title: Pretty goblins / Beth Graham.
Names: Graham, Beth, author.
Description: A play.
Identifiers: Canadiana (print) 20200337769 | Canadiana (ebook) 20200337777 | ISBN 9780369101297 (softcover) | ISBN 9780369101303 (PDF) | ISBN 9780369101310 (EPUB) | ISBN 9780369101327 (Kindle)
Classification: LCC PS8613.R343 P74 2020 | DDC C812/.6—dc23

Playwrights Canada Press operates on Mississaugas of the Credit, Wendat, Anishinaabe, Métis, and Haudenosaunee land. It always was and always will be Indigenous land.

We acknowledge the financial support of the Canada Council for the Arts—which last year invested $153 million to bring the arts to Canadians throughout the country—the Ontario Arts Council (OAC), Ontario Creates, and the Government of Canada for our publishing activities.

Canada Council for the Arts | Conseil des arts du Canada

ONTARIO ARTS COUNCIL
CONSEIL DES ARTS DE L'ONTARIO
an Ontario government agency
un organisme du gouvernement de l'Ontario

Canada

ONTARIO CREATES | ONTARIO CRÉATIF

Pretty Goblins was first produced by Workshop West Playwrights' Theatre and performed at the Backstage Theatre in Edmonton, Alberta, from April 18 to April 29, 2018, with the following cast and creative team:

Laura: Nadien Chu
Lizzie: Miranda Allen

Director: Brian Dooley
Dramaturg: Colleen Murphy
Set, Light, and Costume Designer: Megan Koshka
Sound Design: Jason Kodie
Stage Manager: Erin Valentine
Technical Director: Chris Aasen

CHARACTERS

Laura
Lizzie

LAURA, wearing a coat, opens the door to LIZZIE's apartment. For a moment, she stands at the threshold, framed in the doorway. She sniffs the air.

LAURA: Ugh.

Her gaze sweeps the room and comes to rest on the bed. She shakes her head in disbelief.

Oh my god.

She sets her purse down and inspects the rest of the room, opening a dresser drawer, running her hand over a chair, picking up items on the table, etc. The apartment and its contents are a lot for LAURA to take in. She makes her way over to the bed. LAURA touches the covers, strokes the pillow. She discovers a book (a collection of poems) on or by the bed.

No way.

She reads the front cover. She opens the book and reads an inscription written inside.

. . .

She turns to a page with a torn corner and stares at the text.

(reading aloud) Morning and evening
Maids heard the goblins cry:
"Come buy our orchard fruits,
Come buy, come buy:"

LIZZIE has emerged, unseen by LAURA. LAURA continues reciting the poem from memory.

(by heart) "Apples and quinces,
Lemons and oranges,"

BOTH: *"Plump unpeck'd cherries,*
Melons and raspberries,"

LAURA: Lizzie?

LIZZIE: *"Bloom-down-cheek'd peaches*
Swart-headed mulberries"

Swart-headed. Ya gotta love ye olde English.

LAURA: Lizard!

LIZZIE: Ta da!

LAURA: You're here.

LIZZIE: No shit.

LAURA: You—you look . . .

LIZZIE: Beyond terrible.

LAURA: No, no, you look okay.

LIZZIE: Okay? Wow, you really know how to make a gal feel good about her personal appearance.

LAURA: I mean, you look the same as ever.

LIZZIE: You're diggin' yourself deeper.

LAURA: What the hell am I supposed to say?

LIZZIE: Oh I don't know, that you're happy to see me?

LAURA: I am!

LAURA hugs LIZZIE.

I really am.

LIZZIE: That's more like it.

LAURA: I missed you like stink, ya dink.

LIZZIE: If I'd known you were gonna show up like this, I would've tidied up.

LAURA: There's no windows in here.

LIZZIE: Who needs 'em.

LAURA: I figured you, of all people, would want to see the sky.

LIZZIE: Sky's overrated.

LAURA: And it reeks.

LIZZIE: Home sweet home.

LAURA: Look what I found. *The Book of Poems.*

LAURA turns to the torn page.

The page is torn. Did you do that?

LIZZIE: Just the corner—by accident.

LAURA: You're lucky Mom isn't around. She'd've given you shit.

LIZZIE: *(imitating their mother)* "You wreck everything, you ungrateful little twat!"

LAURA laughs.

LAURA: Twat. She had such a way with words.

LAURA returns to the book.

"Goblin Market." Her favourite.

LIZZIE: Mine too.

LAURA: Ours.

"Wild free-born cranberries"

BOTH: *"Apricots, strawberries—"*

LAURA: Hey! Remember our bedroom at the farmhouse? How we could reach out and hold hands from our beds?

LIZZIE: Oh god yeah! And that ugly wallpaper!

LAURA: *"All ripe together"*

BOTH: *"In the summer weather—"*

LAURA: It's all coming back.

The past. LAURA and LIZZIE are in their farmhouse bedroom. It's the middle of the night.

(nine years old) Lizzie? Are you awake? Lizard!?

LIZZIE: *(nine years old, waking up)* Hm?

LAURA: Wake up!

LIZZIE: What?

LAURA: I had a bad dream.

LIZZIE: So?

LAURA: I'm comin' in.

LAURA climbs into bed with LIZZIE.

LIZZIE: You squirm too much!

LAURA: Something was chasing me and I couldn't run fast enough. It was growling right in my ears.

LIZZIE: Your feet are cold.

LAURA: Quick! Pull the blankets tight so nothing can get us.

They pull the blankets tight and LAURA settles in.

Tell me a story.

LIZZIE: Ask Mom. She's the storyteller.

LAURA: I can't. It's late and she's got the stumbles.

LIZZIE: Uh oh.

LAURA: She called me a fuck up and a waste of space.

LIZZIE: She says the same stuff to me all the time.

LAURA: It hurts my feelings.

LIZZIE: Ignore her. She's a son of a bitch.

LAURA: Lizzie!

LIZZIE: She should know better.

LAURA: She's not always like that. Last week she baked us that cake, remember?

LIZZIE: For dinner.

LAURA: Angel food with sprinkles. Yum.

LIZZIE: She ripped it apart with her hands and plopped it on our plates. Cake blobs. Makes me gag just thinkin' about it.

LAURA: You ate it.

LIZZIE: Cuz I didn't want her to get upset.

LAURA: It was nice. She was wearing lipstick and singing.

LIZZIE: Yeah, and the next day when we came home from school she was still in her nightgown with her hair sticking out, sitting in the corner.

LAURA: I don't know what to do when she's like that.

LIZZIE: Hide!

LAURA: I hate it.

LIZZIE starts to climb out of bed.

LIZZIE: Hey! I know what'll make you feel better.

LAURA: Don't leave me!

LIZZIE: I'm not. I'm gonna show you somethin' real cool.

LAURA: I don't want you to show me anything. I want you to tell me a story.

LIZZIE: You gotta see this. Trust me.

LAURA: Wait!

LAURA picks up the pillow.

You need a pillow if you're gonna step on the floor.

LIZZIE: Huh?

LAURA: There's monsters under the bed. You don't wanna wake 'em up.

LIZZIE: You're a lunatic.

LAURA: Use the pillow, it'll muffle your footsteps!

LIZZIE: Whatever you say, weirdo.

LIZZIE takes the pillow and throws it on the floor, then steps from the bed to the pillow to get to her bag.

LAURA: Hurry up!

LIZZIE: Hold your horses!

LAURA: A monster's gonna / get you.

LIZZIE: Would you shuddup about the monsters?

LAURA: Lizzie!

LIZZIE: You're such a pussy!

LAURA: Hey! Don't call me that.

LIZZIE: Pussy.

LAURA: Get back into bed!

LIZZIE pulls out a tin can and flashlight.

LIZZIE: Got it!

LAURA: Right now!

LIZZIE: Relax.

LIZZIE hops back into bed and holds up the tin can and flashlight for LAURA to see.

Here it is! The solar system.

LAURA: It is not.

LIZZIE: Is too.

LIZZIE places the flashlight in the tin can.

LAURA: Come on! Tell me a story.

She turns on the flashlight. A solar system appears on the ceiling and walls of the bedroom.

LIZZIE: Ta da!

LAURA: Stars!

LIZZIE: I made it in Mr. Alton's science class. I took a map of the solar system and glued it to the top of a coffee can. Then, I took a hammer and a nail and pounded holes in the can wherever the stars were on the map.

LAURA: Wish I had Mr. Alton, but they never put us together. Hold it steady.

LIZZIE: There's Ursa Major—the Big Bear.

LAURA: Where?

LIZZIE: You gotta find the brightest star in the sky—that's the North Star, which is at the end of the handle of the Little Dipper.

LAURA: There?

LIZZIE: Yep. Now, imagine that the Little Dipper is pouring into the Big Dipper. The Big Dipper is the tail of Ursa Major.

LAURA: They all look the same to me.

LIZZIE: Across from the big bear is Gemini—the twins.

LAURA: Like us! Fraternal or identical?

LIZZIE: Identical—

LAURA: Boo.

LIZZIE: I'm gonna see those stars up close one day. In a spaceship. I'm gonna be an astronaut.

LAURA: Me too.

LIZZIE: We'll go on a mission together.

LAURA: All the way to the moon.

LIZZIE: Or even farther.

LAURA: Mars!

LIZZIE: Imagine if we saw a shooting star right now.

LAURA: Not gonna happen with a man-made tin-can solar system.

LIZZIE: Girl-made.

LAURA: Not gonna happen with a girl-made tin-can solar system.

LIZZIE: I know, but it's fun to imagine a star might shoot across our ceiling right this very second.

Whoosh! There goes one! Quick! Make a wish.

LAURA: I wish you'd tell me a story.

LIZZIE: Okaaay, geez, your wish is granted, whiney baby butt.

LAURA: Yes!

LIZZIE: "The Tale of the Hoodelee / Doodelee"!

LAURA: Doodelee! I love that one!

LIZZIE: Over nine years ago, when Mom was pregnant with us, she had to go to the doctor all the time, because having twins is extremely dangerous.

LAURA: We coulda been born dead.

LIZZIE: Whenever Mom went to the doctor,

LAURA: Dad always went with her.

LIZZIE: Mom was so big Dad had to help her get into a special chair

LAURA: so the doctor could rub a goopy-poopy potion all over her great, big baby belly.

LIZZIE: The potion was cold!

LAURA: Brrrr!

LIZZIE: And it tickled!

LIZZIE tickles LAURA.

LAURA: Ah! Stop!

LIZZIE: Then, the doctor would take a magic wand and wave it overtop of Mom's baby belly—

LAURA: Abracadabra!

LIZZIE: And a movie of her insides would appear on a TV screen.

LAURA: Poof!

LIZZIE: Now, guess what they saw on the magic TV?

LAURA: Twins! Me and you! Not one but two!

LIZZIE: Two little twin girl fetuses, floating around in their own pee and poo, way, way up inside their mom's hoodelee doodelee.

LAURA: It's called a vagina.

LIZZIE: D-uh. But the story is "The Tale of the Hoodelee Doodelee," *not* "The Tale of the Vagina," ya dink.

LAURA: I know that, / I was just—

LIZZIE: Do you want me to tell the tale or what?

LAURA: *(chanting)* Tell it! Tell it! / Tell it!

LIZZIE: Now, one of those little twin girl fetuses would become—

LAURA: Baby Lizzie!

LIZZIE: And the other?

LAURA: Baby Laura!

LIZZIE: At every single visit, the doctor listened carefully to Mom's insides—

LAURA: With a magic, uh, thingamabob.

LIZZIE: Stethoscope. And each time the doctor listened he could only hear—

BOTH: One heartbeat!

They make the heartbeat.

Whooshwhoosh

LAURA: / whooshwhoosh,

LIZZIE: because our two hearts were beating together at the exact / same time.

LAURA: Same time!

LIZZIE: But the magic didn't end there.

LAURA: No, siree!

LIZZIE: You see, there was a super duper magic visit, which took place weeks before the twins were even born.

LAURA: On this visit, Mom and Dad and the doctor saw something they'd never seen before up on the TV screen.

LIZZIE: In fact, nobody in the world had ever seen what they saw.

LAURA: It was a scientific phenomenon.

LIZZIE: The two little twin girl fetuses were holding hands!

LAURA: Holding hands!

LIZZIE: Way, way up inside their mother's hoodelee doodelee!

BOTH: Whooshwhoosh whooshwhoosh.

A shift into the present. LIZZIE's apartment.

LAURA: Oh god, we were so little.

LIZZIE: Fraternal twins can't hold hands. It's impossible.

LAURA: What am I even doing here?

LIZZIE: Separate amniotic sacs.

LAURA: This is so messed up. This place . . . this book . . . this poem . . .

"Grapes fresh from the vine"

LIZZIE: *"Pomegranates full and fine."*

The past.

LAURA: *(ten years old)* Hey! I know you took it! Give it back!

LIZZIE: *(ten years old)* I don't know what you're talking about.

LAURA: My cherry Lip Smacker! You stole it!

LIZZIE: Did not.

LAURA catches her.

LAURA: Liar! I saw you with it at recess.

LIZZIE: I didn't steal it.

LAURA pries it out of LIZZIE's hand.

LAURA: Oh yeah? Then what's this?

LIZZIE: I borrowed it.

LAURA: Without asking. That's stealing.

LIZZIE: I needed Lip Smacker.

LAURA: To play that stupid game.

LIZZIE: It's called "Boys Chase the Girls," and it's not stupid.

LAURA: It makes no sense.

LIZZIE: It makes perfect sense. If you wanna play you stand in the middle of the field and put Lip Smacker on to let the boys know you're ready. Then they chase after you until they catch you. Those are the rules.

LAURA: Says Stephanie.

LIZZIE: And me.

LAURA: Stephanie's dumb.

LIZZIE: She is not. She's cool.

LAURA: Oh, so that's why you do everything she says.

LIZZIE: I do not. I made up some of the rules too. They're not all hers.

LAURA: I know what happens when the boys catch the girls. They kiss you. I saw. Yuck! I bet that was one of your rules.

LIZZIE: Here. Have your Lip Smacker back. See if I care.

LAURA: What happened to your hands?

LIZZIE: I fell when Derek was chasing me. I scraped 'em on the ground.

LAURA: Do they hurt?

LIZZIE: Not anymore because Derek kissed them all better when he caught me.

LAURA: Ew.

LIZZIE: And then I kissed him back, hard, on the lips.

LAURA: Barf.

LIZZIE smiles and shrugs.

Oh my god! You like Derek!

LIZZIE: Maybe.

LAURA: I bet you fell on purpose so he would catch you.

LIZZIE: Wouldn't you like to know.

LAURA: That is so sick.

LIZZIE: You're jealous!

LAURA: Of who?

LIZZIE: Derek, because you think I like him better than you.

LAURA: I do not.

LIZZIE: If I don't play, I won't have any friends.

LAURA: Like me.

LIZZIE: You have friends.

LAURA: Who?

LIZZIE: Hello.

LAURA: You're my sister. You don't count. Here. Keep it. Your cooties are all over it anyway.

LIZZIE: Look, I'm sorry I stole your Lip Smacker. Let me make it up to you.

LAURA: How?

LIZZIE: I'll show you how to play the game.

LAURA: No thanks.

LIZZIE: First, let me wipe my cooties off.

LIZZIE takes the cap off the Lip Smacker and wipes it off.

There. Almost gone. Now, you have to wipe it on your lips to get rid of the rest of 'em.

LAURA: That's not how it works.

LIZZIE: Yes, it is. It's one of the rules. Put on the Lip Smacker.

LAURA: . . . ?

LIZZIE: Put it on.

LAURA applies the Lip Smacker.

LAURA: There. Satisfied?

LIZZIE grabs her by the shoulders.

LIZZIE: Ha! Gotcha. The boy catches the girl.

LAURA: But I wasn't trying / to run—

LIZZIE: Too late. You put on the Lip Smacker. You gave the signal.

LAURA: But I didn't know / that we were—

LIZZIE: Shhhh! I caught you.

LAURA: But—

LIZZIE: Close your eyes.

LAURA: What?

LIZZIE: Rules! Close 'em!

LAURA closes her eyes. LIZZIE kisses her.

And that's how the game is played.

LAURA: Weird.

LIZZIE: I think it's fun.

LAURA: You would.

LAURA wipes off her mouth.

LIZZIE: Next time, I'll give you the tongue.

LAURA: Gross! Have you?

LIZZIE: Once or twice.

LAURA: Whoa.

LIZZIE: You could play with us if you wanted.

LAURA: No way.

LIZZIE: Suit yourself.

LAURA: . . . Do you?

LIZZIE: Do I what?

LAURA: Like Derek better than me.

LIZZIE: No. Derek's just a boy. You're my sister. I belong to you and you belong to me.

A shift into the present. LIZZIE*'s apartment.*

LAURA: You belong to me and I belong to you.

They crouch close together.

Derek!

LIZZIE: *In the cooling weather,*

BOTH: *With clasping hands and cautioning—*

LAURA: Fucking Derek!

The past. LAURA *and* LIZZIE *are in the bathroom at the farmhouse.*

(thirteen years old) Oh no, we used all the hot water. Mom's gonna be pissed.

LIZZIE: *(thirteen years old, doing an imitation of their mother)* "You two little shits, how do you expect me to keep my hoodelee doodelee clean for your father?"

LAURA: Ew.

LIZZIE: *(continuing the imitation)* "It's like a grilled cheese sandwich down there."

LAURA: Hold still! The package says I'm supposed to work the cream all the way from your scalp to the ends of your hair.

LIZZIE: I wonder what it's made of, cuz it looked like jizz when you were squeezing it outta the bottle.

LAURA: It did?

LIZZIE: Maybe that's the secret ingredient.

LAURA: I sincerely hope not.

LIZZIE: Whatever. Lots of stuff looks like jizz. What's this gunk supposed to do anyway?

LAURA: It deep conditions and adds volume.

LIZZIE: Oooh la la.

LAURA: Leaving your hair shiny and soft.

LIZZIE: Derek won't be able to keep his hands offa me.

LAURA: He already can't.

LIZZIE: . . . Something happened to me today.

LAURA: So? Something happens to everyone every day.

LIZZIE: Something significant, ya boob.

LAURA: Like what?

LIZZIE: Lemme show ya.

LIZZIE stands up and faces LAURA.

LAURA: Wait! Don't get out! I'm not done with your hair.

LIZZIE: Shuddup for a second and watch the water.

LAURA: What for?

LIZZIE: Eyes on the water, pervert.

LAURA: I'm not the pervert. You're the one talking about jizz!

LIZZIE: Eyes! Water! Now!

LAURA: . . .

LIZZIE: All right.

LAURA: I don't see any/thing.

LIZZIE: Wait for it.

LAURA: . . .

LIZZIE: . . .

LAURA sighs.

Wait.

LAURA burbles her lips.

Keep watching.

LAURA: I am.

LIZZIE: . . .

LAURA: . . .

LIZZIE: There! See that?

LAURA: Blood!

LIZZIE: From my hoodelee doodelee.

LAURA: You got your period!

LIZZIE: In math class. Had to wad up a bunch of toilet paper and stick it in my gitch until I got home.

LAURA: You're a woman!

LIZZIE: Whatever that means.

LAURA: Means you can get pregnant.

LIZZIE: *If* I was having sex.

LAURA: You practically are.

LIZZIE: Am not!

LAURA: From what you told me, I'd say you're pretty close.

LIZZIE: He's not sticking it in me.

LAURA: Yet.

LIZZIE: I'm not a slut.

LAURA: I never said you were. Mom did.

LIZZIE: She calls everybody that.

LAURA: Slut!

LIZZIE: Whore!

LAURA: Floozy!

LIZZIE: Town bike!

LAURA: Skanky jizzface slaghole dong-sucking sperm dumpster!

LIZZIE: You win.

LAURA: . . . Do you feel any different?

LIZZIE: Yeah, I got major cramps, and if I close my eyes, I swear, I can envision the exact shape of my uterus.

LAURA: Wow.

LIZZIE: Being on the rag makes you super aware of your lady parts. Hurry up and finish my hair before I bleed out in the tub.

LAURA: Not funny.

LIZZIE: It could happen, you know.

LAURA: Liar.

LIZZIE: You should never take a hot bath when you're having your period. It's extremely dangerous. Women have died.

LAURA: . . . Seriously?

LIZZIE laughs.

LIZZIE: Gotcha!

LAURA: Bitch.

LAURA punches her.

LIZZIE: Ow!

The laugh settles.

LAURA: How you gonna have your period in outer space?

LIZZIE: Same way Valentina Tereshkova and Roberta Bondar did. It flows the same direction in space as it does on earth, right out of the hoodelee doodelee and into the atmosphere.

LAURA: Wouldn't it float back up inside you?

LIZZIE: Nope. Lady blood defies gravity. So does poop, at least when it's inside the human body. It's once it's out that it becomes a problem. Microgravity can make things messy. Did you know Buzz Aldrin chased a piece of his own poop around a spacecraft with a plastic bag? Took him hours to catch it.

LIZZIE pretends to float a piece of poo at LAURA's face.

LAURA: Ah! Get that outta my face!

LIZZIE makes a crackling noise as if talking over the radio in a space helmet.

LIZZIE: Apollo 17 to mission control.

LAURA makes a crackling noise as if talking over the radio in a space helmet.

LAURA: Go ahead, Apollo.

LIZZIE: I've got a rogue shit aboard my shuttle—I'm gonna have to make an emergency landing.

LAURA: Permission to initiate descent.

LIZZIE: Burn complete. Entering atmosphere. Heat shield jettisoned. Parachute deployed.

LAURA: Apollo 17, please confirm touchdown.

LIZZIE: Touchdown confirmed. Apollo 17 has landed, but I'm afraid the rogue shit has wreaked havoc. I'm gonna need a clean-up crew out here pronto.

LAURA stops pretending to talk over a radio.

LAURA: Lizzie, I don't want you to go into outer space. It's too far away.

LIZZIE: I gotta explore the unknown, gotta search for my place in the universe.

LAURA: But—

LIZZIE: "Man must rise above the earth—to the top of the atmosphere and beyond—for only thus will he understand the world in which he lives." Socrates said that.

LAURA: I don't care who said what. I don't want you to go. You might get lost out there.

LIZZIE: Then you'll have to come find me.

LAURA: Mission control to Captain Lizard, I need your coordinates.

LIZZIE makes a radio crackle.

LIZZIE: *"We must not look at goblin men"*

LAURA: Earth to Lizard.

LIZZIE makes a radio crackle.

LIZZIE: *"We must not buy their fruits:"*

LAURA: Please come in.

LIZZIE makes a radio crackle.

A shift into the present. LIZZIE's apartment.

Lizard, do you read me?

LIZZIE: . . .

LAURA: Lizzie?

LIZZIE: . . .

LAURA: *"Who knows upon what soil they fed*
Their hungry thirsty roots?"

The past. LAURA *and* LIZZIE *are in their kitchen at the farmhouse. Something like "Just A Girl" by No Doubt plays on the radio.*

(fifteen years old) Whoo! He's gone! Dad is gonzo!

LIZZIE: *(fifteen years old)* You positive?

LAURA: Hundred percent. I watched his truck turn out the driveway onto the highway and disappear from sight.

LIZZIE: What about Mom?

LAURA: She called from Auntie Jo's. Says she's gonna crash there.

LIZZIE: Yes! The house is ours!

LAURA: You got the empty bottle?

LIZZIE *holds up a jar.*

LIZZIE: Yo.

LAURA: A pickle jar?!

LIZZIE: It was all I could find.

LAURA: Get the booze.

LIZZIE: On it. Oh my god! I love this song.

LAURA: Fuck yeah!

LIZZIE *starts pulling out bottles.*

LIZZIE: Booze. Booze. Booze. And more booze.

LAURA: Good. Now, we skim a little from each bottle.

LIZZIE and LAURA start pouring.

Not too much, we don't want Mom to figure it out.

LIZZIE: She won't.

LAURA: If it looks obvious, we replace it with water.

LIZZIE: She's not gonna figure it out!

LAURA sips from a bottle of crème de menthe.

LAURA: Minty!

LIZZIE sips from a bottle of bourbon.

LIZZIE: Gah! Not minty at all!

LAURA: Do you wanna get blatto?

LIZZIE: Oh yeah!

LAURA: I said, do you wanna get blatto?

LIZZIE: Oh yeeaah! Blattoblattoblatto, baby!

LAURA: And now for the pièce de résistance. Le pop de l'orange!

LAURA adds some orange pop.

Voila.

LAURA sips and gags.

Ugh. Shit mix with a hint of dill. Take a swig.

LIZZIE: Cheers, big ears!

LIZZIE takes a gulp.

LAURA: Call Derek. Tell him to pick us up.

LIZZIE: Unh unh, I'm drivin'.

LAURA: You don't have your licence.

LIZZIE: Got my learner's. Close enough.

LAURA: Anything happens and we are doomed.

LIZZIE: To the minivan, baby!

LAURA: Doomed!

LIZZIE climbs into the minivan.

LIZZIE: All aboard the Boozer Cruiser.

LAURA takes the passenger seat.

LAURA: Dooooomed!

LIZZIE grips the wheel.

LIZZIE: Flight navigation system engaged.

LAURA: Hands at ten and two?

LIZZIE: Check. Go ahead and calculate our desired trajectory.

LAURA: The party's not too far from Rae Anne's. She said we drive past the pond, get out at the dead end, and walk up the path into the trees.

LIZZIE: It's a bush bash, baby!

LAURA: All right, bush party rule number one—stick with me.

LIZZIE: Stick with you.

LAURA: Only smoke what I smoke.

LIZZIE: Smoke 'em if you got 'em.

LAURA: Only drink what we brought.

LIZZIE: The solution is pollution.

LAURA: I think this is the place. Looks like we park over / there.

LIZZIE: Ooo! Bonfire!

LIZZIE screeches to a halt.

LAURA: Or here's fine too.

LIZZIE jumps out of the car.

LIZZIE: Let's get this party started!

LAURA: Wait up!

LIZZIE has taken off. LAURA gets out of the car as LIZZIE throws a sleeping bag around her shoulders.

(calling) Lizzie? Where'd you go?

LIZZIE: Over here by the fire!

She sneaks around behind LAURA.

LAURA: Where?

LIZZIE: Boo!

LAURA: Ah! You fucker.

LIZZIE: Check it out. My superhero cape.

LAURA: It's a sleeping bag.

LIZZIE: Oh no no, this is no ordinary sleeping bag, and I am no ordinary human. I am super bush! Impervious to flame!

LAURA: Don't be an / idiot.

LIZZIE runs around the bonfire.

LIZZIE: Faster than a speeding minivan!

LAURA: Careful!

LIZZIE: Able to leap a bonfire in a single bound!

LAURA: Lizzie, no.

LIZZIE leaps over the bonfire.

LIZZIE: / Whoo!

LAURA: No! Watch out!

LIZZIE leaps over the bonfire again.

LIZZIE: I am invincible!

LAURA: You're gonna / catch on fire!

LIZZIE: Ahhh!

LAURA: Stop, drop, and roll!

LIZZIE rolls around on the ground.

LIZZIE: Ah! Ah! Ah!

She *gets back up, unscathed, laughing.*

Ta da! Told you I was invincible.

LAURA: Holy shit.

LIZZIE: Superbush strikes again! Ugh. I feel . . . ugh . . .

LAURA: Uh oh.

LIZZIE: I think I'm gonna . . .

LIZZIE barfs.

LAURA: Oh no.

LIZZIE: Ugh . . . Whoo! . . . Ugh.

LAURA: Here, lemme hold your hair back.

LIZZIE barfs again, then laughs.

LIZZIE: Don't worry about me, it's just my vestibular system adapting to weightlessness. Ugh. Oh man, I drank too much.

A shift into the present. LIZZIE's apartment.

LAURA: You sure did. Like a fish. Like Mom.

LIZZIE: Like mother, like daughter.

LAURA: *Sweeter than . . . sweeter than . . . ?*

LIZZIE: *honey from the rock*

LAURA: *Stronger than man-rejoicing wine*

The past. LAURA and LIZZIE are at a funeral. Funeral music plays.

(sixteen years old, at her mother's funeral) Whoa. There she is.

LIZZIE: *(sixteen years old)* Sometimes you gotta see it to believe it.

LAURA looks away.

LAURA: Ugh. I can't look at her like this.

LIZZIE: Want me to describe her?

LAURA: No! . . . Yes.

LIZZIE: She's plastered in makeup, but she looks way better than she did right before she croaked—it's like she could sit up and start swearing at us any second.

LAURA: I'm gonna miss her.

LIZZIE: I'm not. She stunk. Especially near the end. Her hospital room was rancid.

LAURA: Shhh.

LIZZIE: Smelled like a putrid dick.

LAURA: Don't say that kinda stuff!

LIZZIE: Must be what death smells like, a putrid / dick—

LAURA: Shuddup!

LIZZIE: Why? Whaddya think, she can hear us?

LAURA: Maybe.

LIZZIE: She's dead.

LAURA: Yeah, but . . .

LIZZIE: Say something to her.

LAURA: Like what?

LIZZIE: I dunno. Something you never got to say to her when she was alive.

LAURA approaches the coffin.

LAURA: Mom? Why?

LIZZIE: . . . You done?

LAURA nods.

My turn.

LIZZIE leans into the coffin.

Fuck you, Mom. Fuck you for every nasty thing you ever said to us, for drinking yourself into oblivion, for dying long before you ever should have. Fuck you.

LAURA: . . .

LIZZIE: . . .

LAURA: . . . Whoa.

LIZZIE: Let's get outta here. Auntie Jo said she'd give us a lift.

LAURA: We should wait for Dad.

LIZZIE: He's gonna take forever.

LAURA: But he needs / us.

LIZZIE: I wanna go. Now!

(calling) Auntie Jo!

LAURA: Wait up!

LIZZIE: Hurry, she's gonna leave without us!

We hear an engine start up. LAURA *and* LIZZIE *climb into the back seat of Auntie Jo's car.*

LAURA: Thanks for the lift, Auntie Jo.

LIZZIE: Yeah, thanks.

LAURA: . . .

LIZZIE pokes LAURA.

LIZZIE: . . . Poke.

LAURA: . . .

LIZZIE: Poke.

LAURA: Don't.

LIZZIE: Poke.

LAURA: Lizzie!

LIZZIE: Poke.

LAURA: Screw off!

LIZZIE: Poke.

LAURA loses it.

LAURA: Urrrgh! What's the matter with you?

LIZZIE: Everything. Poke.

LAURA grabs LIZZIE's hands and squeezes.

LAURA: Leave me alone!

LIZZIE: Or what?

LAURA: I'll beat the living shit out of you.

LAURA lets go of her and gives her a punch.

LIZZIE: Ow! Geez. Mom's dead. Get over it.

LAURA: Like you just did? On the same day as her funeral.

LIZZIE: Yup. Wham. Bam. Over it.

LAURA: Well, I'm not over it! Mom's dead and I'm sad about it! So let me be sad. Just let me be.

LIZZIE: . . .

LAURA: . . .

LIZZIE: Poke.

LAURA: Fuck.

LIZZIE: Pokety poke.

LAURA starts laughing.

It's not me, it's my finger. Poke poke / poke.

LAURA laughs.

LAURA: You're such / a jerk!

LIZZIE: I can't control it. Poke poke poke.

Their laughter settles.

Don't get upset. She's not worth it.

LAURA: Easy for you to say.

LIZZIE: No, it isn't. It's hard for me to say. Really hard.

LAURA rests her head on LIZZIE's shoulder.

Remember when she used to stand on the porch in the middle of the night and howl at the coyotes?

LAURA: Yeah. And they'd howl back.

LIZZIE: Dad would just shake his head and say, "There's nothing you can do when she's like this. You just gotta let her wear herself out." And she would. She'd howl herself hoarse. The call of the wild.

LIZZIE looks out the window of the car and howls quietly.

Aroooo.

LAURA covers her ears.

LAURA: Don't.

LIZZIE: Makes her feel close, like her ghost is listening. Who knows? Maybe the dead can hear the living even if we can't hear them.

A shift into the present. LAURA *uncovers her ears and tries to howl. The attempt is barely audible.*

LAURA: Pathetic.

LIZZIE: Come on, ya chickenshit, throw your head back and let 'er rip.

LAURA *tries to howl again.*

LAURA: I can't.

LIZZIE: Chickenshit.

LAURA *lays down on the bed and stares up at the ceiling.*

LAURA: I . . . I'm not like you.

LIZZIE: You lucked out.

LAURA: *How fair the vine must grow*

BOTH: *Whose grapes are so luscious;*
How warm the wind must blow

The past. LAURA *is in her bed at the farmhouse.* LIZZIE *has just come home.*

LAURA: *(sixteen years old, sitting up in bed)* Where've you been? I woke up and you weren't here. Scared me half to death.

LIZZIE: *(sixteen years old)* I'm fucked up.

LAURA: You reek.

LIZZIE: I'm gonna sleep with you.

LAURA: No. Go sleep it off in your own bed.

LIZZIE: I can't be alone right now.

LAURA: You shoulda thought of that before / you—

LIZZIE: I don't wanna be alone!

LAURA: What's the matter?

LIZZIE: I hurt.

LAURA: You're hurt?

LIZZIE: How?

LAURA: Mmmmm.

LIZZIE winces in pain.

Where?

LIZZIE groans in pain.

Do you need to go to the hospital or something?

LIZZIE: No!

LAURA: What's wrong?

LIZZIE: I should never have gone. I'm so stupid.

LIZZIE hits herself on the head with her open palms.

Stupid.

She hits herself again.

LAURA: Stop that.

LIZZIE: Stupid.

LAURA: Let's wake Dad up.

LIZZIE: No!

LAURA: But you're / hurt.

LIZZIE: No, don't get Dad. I need you to hold me.

LAURA: I am.

LIZZIE: Hold me!

LAURA: I got you.

LIZZIE: Hold me tight.

LAURA: Okay, I got you tight.

LIZZIE: Tighter.

LAURA: If I hold you any tighter, your head's gonna pop off.

LIZZIE: Don't look at me.

LAURA: Why can't / I look.

LIZZIE: Just don't. Look away.

LAURA: Okay, I'm not looking at you.

LIZZIE groans.

Lizard, you're freaking me out. What's happened?

LIZZIE: Hold me, don't look at me, and listen.

LAURA: I'm doing all of those things. Please, tell me what's going on.

LIZZIE: I should never have gone to Derek's.

LAURA: You go to his place all the time.

LIZZIE: Not tonight! I shouldn't have gone tonight!

LAURA: Why not?

LIZZIE: His older brother was there with his friends. They were drinking. I was drinking. All of us were. He told me and Derek if we came downstairs he'd smoke us up. Only Derek didn't go downstairs. I went by myself.

LAURA: Why didn't he go with you?

LIZZIE: Cuz he's a fucking coward! I followed Derek's brother's friend into a room and . . . and then he pushed me down on the floor and . . .

She whimpers.

LAURA: He raped you.

LIZZIE nods.

LIZZIE: Yeah.

LAURA: Oh, Lizard. No.

LIZZIE: Yeah, he . . . they . . . did.

LAURA: We should get Dad.

LIZZIE: No! I don't want him to know.

LAURA: We gotta tell somebody.

LIZZIE: I don't want anyone to know.

LAURA: The police.

LIZZIE: No way. Nonono. They'll just . . . Come on. A girl at a party with a bunch of boys? Drinking? Smoking weed? It was stupid. I shouldn't have gotten so messed up.

LAURA: You couldn't have known they'd do that.

LIZZIE: I was partying hard.

LAURA: It wasn't your fault.

LIZZIE: Laura? I'm having my period.

LAURA: Good. I hope they're covered in it.

LIZZIE: No. No, I had a—I was wearing a tampon.

LAURA: Oh.

LIZZIE: And it's—it's—

LAURA: Still inside you.

LIZZIE nods.

Oh god, Lizard.

LIZZIE: You gotta help me.

LAURA: Let's go to the hospital.

LIZZIE: No. I told you—

LAURA: But, / Lizzie—

LIZZIE: I can't. I won't.

LAURA: What about Auntie Jo? She could be here in ten minutes.

LIZZIE: No.

LAURA: But she's a nurse.

LIZZIE: Don't. She'll kick my ass. I need you and only you. Help me, please.

LAURA: How?

LIZZIE: I wanna take a bath.

LAURA: Okay.

LIZZIE: But first I need you to take my pants and underwear off because I can't do it by myself. And I need you to help me take it out—the tampon.

LAURA: . . . Okay.

First your shoes.

LAURA kneels in front of LIZZIE.

There's one. There's the other. Good. Now your socks.

And your pants. Good. Okay . . . next is your underwear.

LIZZIE: Go for it.

LAURA: Now . . . now, I'm gonna try to find it. You ready?

LIZZIE takes a deep breath in.

LIZZIE: I'm ready.

LAURA: Okay, here we go.

LIZZIE winces when LAURA touches her.

Sorry.

LIZZIE: Your hands are cold.

LAURA: Sorry.

LIZZIE grunts in pain.

I'm so sorry.

LIZZIE grunts in pain.

I'm trying to be gentle, it's just—

LIZZIE: I know. Keep going.

LAURA: Breathe and try to relax your muscles.

LIZZIE breathes deeply.

Good.

LIZZIE keeps breathing deeply.

There it is. I got the string.

LIZZIE: Get it out.

LAURA: Okay . . . Okay. Push.

LIZZIE grunts.

That's it. Keep breathing.

LIZZIE breathes.

And push again.

LIZZIE grunts.

That's it.

LIZZIE grunts.

There. It's out. You did it.

LIZZIE: Fuck, I hurt.

LAURA wraps up the tampon and throws it in the garbage.

LAURA: I'll run you a bath and I'll wash your back.

LIZZIE: Just like Mom used to. I wish she was here right now.

LAURA: Me too.

LIZZIE: She'd tell me to howl it out.

LIZZIE howls. The sound is strangled, not fully formed, awful. LIZZIE's howl dissolves into tears, which she fights back.

Fuck this! Where's that tampon?

LAURA: I threw it in the trash.

LIZZIE: Find a pen and paper.

LAURA: What for?

LIZZIE digs through the trash.

LIZZIE: I gotta send a message.

LAURA looks for a pen and paper.

LAURA: To who?

LIZZIE: Find that pen and paper and I'll tell you.

LAURA: What are you . . . ?

LIZZIE: Hurry up.

LIZZIE finds the tampon.

Got it!

LAURA: Pen. Paper. Here.

LIZZIE: Write this down.

(dictating) Dear Andy . . . and the gang, you left your sperm behind.

LAURA stares at LIZZIE, jaw agape.

What are you waiting for? Write.

LAURA: *(as she writes)* You left your sperm behind.

LIZZIE: I soaked it up as best I could with my lady plug . . . but I got no use for it, so take it back and shove it up your own hole . . . Suck it, assholes.

LAURA: *(writing)* . . . Suck it, assholes.

LIZZIE: From . . . from who?

LAURA: Superbush.

LIZZIE: Perfect.

LIZZIE looks around.

You know that instruction sheet that comes in the tampon box?

LAURA: Yeah.

LIZZIE: Where is it?

LAURA: Still in the box, I think.

LIZZIE digs through the trash again.

LIZZIE: Ha! Got it!

She gives the instruction sheet to LAURA.

Here. Circle and underline the part where it tells you how to insert the tampon.

LAURA: Done and done.

LIZZIE: Now write "Foreplay" above it. In caps.

LAURA: Oh shit, that's good.

LIZZIE: Put it all in an envelope and deliver it.

LAURA: Who? Me?

LIZZIE: You're the only one I trust.

A shift into the present. LIZZIE's apartment.

LAURA: I delivered it to Derek the next day. Put the package right in his hand, watched him open it and told him to make sure to pass it on to Andy and his friends. You shoulda seen the look on his face.

LIZZIE chuckles.

LIZZIE: I can only imagine.

LAURA: You and I were different after that. Changed.

The past. LAURA and LIZZIE stand on the porch of the farm-house. LIZZIE wears a backpack.

(seventeen years old) Please, don't go.

LIZZIE: *(seventeen years old)* I have to.

LAURA: Don't leave me.

LIZZIE: Laura.

LAURA: We're not even finished high school yet. There's only a couple months left.

LIZZIE: I'm failing four classes.

LAURA: You could still turn it around.

LIZZIE: Mrs. Dumaine already told me I'm not gonna graduate. I'll have to repeat the semester, and I'm not about to spend any more time in that hellhole. Fuck that.

LAURA: But you're all I've got.

LIZZIE: This isn't about you.

LAURA: No, it's about *us*.

LIZZIE: It's about me. There's too much history in this place. I have to get away from it for a while.

LAURA: Dad's really angry.

LIZZIE: He's gonna have to suck it up.

LAURA: He doesn't understand.

LIZZIE: Don't say a fucking word to him about this.

LAURA: But, maybe if you—

LIZZIE: Laura, listen to me! Because I don't want to have to say this again, ever. There's an anniversary coming up. It'll be one year since Andy and the gang, and there's no way I'm sticking around for that, because one day I wanna be able to pull my pants down to take a piss without shaking like a leaf, understand?

LAURA: . . .

LIZZIE: If I don't get out of here, I'll never get over what happened!

LAURA: . . . Is that all you're taking with you?

LIZZIE: It's all I need. If I forgot something, I'll get you to bring it when you come to visit me in the big city.

LAURA: It's not that big.

LIZZIE: In the medium-sized city then. Better?

LAURA: More accurate.

LIZZIE: Dink.

LAURA: I'm gonna miss you.

LIZZIE: Ditto. I'm only a two-hour bus ride away. I'll send you an address once I get set up, okay?

LAURA: Okay.

LIZZIE: Come on, this is an adventure.

LAURA: Your ride's here.

LIZZIE: I gotta go.

LAURA: Call me as soon as you get there.

LIZZIE: I will. I'll give you a full report.

A car horn honks.

See ya!

LAURA: G'bye.

LIZZIE: Coming!

A shift into the present. LIZZIE*'s apartment.*

LAURA: It was so hard to watch you go.

Like two pigeons in one nest

LIZZIE: *Folded in each other's wings*

I needed a clean slate.

LAURA: We both did.

The past. LIZZIE *is visiting* LAURA.

(twenty years old, chanting) This is your birthday song!

LIZZIE: *(twenty years old, chanting back)* It won't take very long—

BOTH: Did it!

LAURA: You brought cupcakes!

LIZZIE: Oh shit, I forgot the candles.

LAURA: We'll make do without.

LIZZIE: Whoo! The big two-oh.

LAURA: Oh god, we're old.

LIZZIE: No way, baby. We still got a lotta livin' to do.

LAURA: Make a wish.

They both close their eyes.

LIZZIE: Whatcha wishin' for?

LAURA: Not tellin'.

LIZZIE: Me neither.

LAURA: Gotta keep it a secret or it won't come true.

LIZZIE: Wishin' complete.

LIZZIE opens her eyes and takes in the place.

I like the new pad.

LAURA: Me too. It's closer to the university. Last term I was so far away, took me forever to get home. Drink?

LIZZIE: Abso-frickin-lutely!

LAURA: Comin' right up.

LIZZIE: How'd the exams go?

LAURA: Biology 204 was a bitch but the rest of 'em went okay. You?

LIZZIE: I'm so close to having my high school. All I got left is math. Then I can apply for university.

LAURA: Excellent.

LIZZIE: You're not gonna be the only one taking a Bachelor of Science.

LAURA toasts.

LAURA: Cheers, big ears!

LIZZIE: *Nostrovia*! That means "to your health" in Russian. The language of the stars. It's a requirement for international space flight. I bought a phrase book. *Zemli*—that means "earth."

LAURA: *Zemli.*

LIZZIE: Keep workin' on it. Hey, you still creamin' your jeans over that dude with the curly hair?

LAURA: His name's David. We've been seeing quite a bit of each other lately.

LIZZIE: Oh yeah? What bits have you seen?

LAURA: And here I thought turning twenty would make you more mature.

LIZZIE: *(imitating LAURA)* Oh, Dave, you're such a genius and your pheromones are out of this world. Oh, Daaave.

LAURA: David.

LIZZIE: David. That name is so vanilla.

LAURA: I like it.

LIZZIE: So, have you?

LAURA: . . . Have I what?

LIZZIE: Oh my god, you have! You totally have!

LAURA: How can you tell?

LIZZIE: A sister always knows. Why didn't you report back immediately?

LAURA: Because it's private! And because I knew I was going to see you and I wanted to tell you in person.

LIZZIE: How was it?

LAURA: Uh. Do you really wanna hear about my sex life?

LIZZIE: I do, actually. I really do. I wanna know what it was like for you.

LAURA: Uh, he knew I was nervous, so we took it real slow. He cooked dinner and we had a bath together and then we made out, got into bed, and then we . . . you know . . . did it.

LIZZIE: You made love.

LAURA: I guess.

LIZZIE: Sounds like that's what it was.

LAURA: Honestly, the actual event was kinda awkward and uncomfortable and messy. But, get this, he laid out a towel, just in case I bled.

LIZZIE: Holy shit, man, chivalry is not dead. That David of yours is a keeper.

LAURA: He is.

LIZZIE: It's nice to hear it can be good.

LAURA: It can. It really can.

LIZZIE: Wouldn't know, never done it sober.

LAURA: Maybe you just gotta find the right guy.

LIZZIE: It ain't Roger, that's for sure.

LAURA: Roger?

LIZZIE: He's a regular at the bar. He always sits in my section, buys me drinks while I serve him. We flirt and one thing leads to another. It's meaningless.

LAURA: Hm.

LIZZIE: He's the night manager's husband.

LAURA: Oh shit.

LIZZIE: The booze made me do it. That'll be my excuse.

LAURA: We don't have to drink tonight. You want a pop?

LIZZIE: No way, it's our birthday and I wanna party with my twin sister.

LIZZIE picks up a bottle and pours them both a drink.

LIZZIE toasts.

Let's get blatto!

LIZZIE passes the drink to LAURA.

To Laura and Lizzie! Cheers!

LAURA doesn't drink.

A shift into the present. LIZZIE's apartment.

LAURA: Cheers, big ears.

LAURA doesn't drink.

LIZZIE: *Nostrovia.*

LAURA doesn't drink.

LAURA: To Laura and . . .

LIZZIE: Lizzie.

LAURA doesn't drink.

LAURA: Blatto blatto blatto.

LIZZIE: Never leave a bottle unfinished.

LAURA sets the drink down.

The past, after LAURA's graduation ceremony. LIZZIE is tipsy.

LAURA: *(twenty-three years old)* Thanks for sitting through that endless ceremony.

LIZZIE: *(twenty-three years old)* You're a Bachelor of Science now, baby! It's official.

LAURA: Yeah, now I can officially turn around and go right back to school. Next up, lab tech. Stool samples, here I come!

LIZZIE: I can't believe you actually wanna look at poo through a microscope for a living.

LAURA: Not just poo. Blood, snot, saliva, all kinds of bodily fluids.

LIZZIE: Did you hear me cheer when you walked across the stage?

LAURA: Everyone heard you.

LIZZIE: I couldn't help myself. I was proud. David looked like he wanted the seat to swallow him up when I did it.

LAURA: He's an introvert.

LIZZIE: Dad cried.

LAURA: He did?

LIZZIE: It was sweet. But what's with that new girlfriend of his?

LAURA: Marilyn.

LIZZIE: Yeah, Marilyn. She was all over him, hugging and cooing and holding his hand.

LAURA: Dad asked for an extra ticket. I thought it was for Auntie Jo and then surprise! He shows up to my graduation with a date.

LIZZIE: Her laugh sounds like a machine gun, and she's got huge bazoongas.

LAURA: Oh come on, she seems nice enough.

LIZZIE: She seems boring. Not a drop of coyote blood. Nothin' like Mom.

LAURA: Maybe that's a good thing. I think Dad likes her—a lot.

LIZZIE: The dude is smitten.

LAURA: You comin' to dinner?

LIZZIE: For a bit. I'm trying to avoid the whole party thing. Don't wanna be tempted. Three months since I've had a drink!

LAURA: If you don't count this afternoon.

LIZZIE: I'm failing calculus. I gotta hit the books. If I can't get through a first-year class, how am I gonna get through the next three years? I used to be so good in school.

LAURA: And you will be again. You're just out of practice. I could help.

LIZZIE: You're too busy.

LAURA: Better yet, I'll ask David.

LIZZIE: He's even busier. He's not gonna wanna—

LAURA: I'll tell him he has to. For my sake.

LIZZIE: I don't want your charity.

LAURA: That's not what this is. David'll want to help. Trust me, he loves being a hero.

LIZZIE: He loves you.

LAURA: That too.

LIZZIE: Laura saves the day.

LAURA: David saves the day. It'll be a cinch for him. The guy's a math genius. He dreams in numbers.

LIZZIE: Okay, fine, but I wanna be the one to ask him.

LAURA: Uh, maybe / wait.

LIZZIE: Yo, David! Can ya help a future sister-in-law out?

A shift into the present. LIZZIE's apartment.

LAURA: Oh. Shit.

LIZZIE: David.

LAURA: Yeah. David.

"Did you miss me?"

BOTH: *"Come and kiss me"*

LAURA: *"Never mind my bruises"*

The past. An overly romantic love song plays. LAURA *and* LIZZIE *are at their father's wedding.* LIZZIE *is tipsy once again. They watch their father and Marilyn dancing on the dance floor.*

(twenty-seven years old) Wow. Marilyn and Dad gettin' hitched. They could not have picked a cheesier song for their first dance.

LIZZIE: *(twenty-seven years old)* It's a wedding. Everything's cheesy when it comes to holy matrimony.

LAURA: Well, if it makes him happy—

LIZZIE: Gag.

LAURA: —and he seems happy—

LIZZIE: Barf.

LAURA: —then who are we to say?

LIZZIE: We're his daughters, for fuck's sake! He coulda asked our permission.

LAURA: Dads don't need permission.

LIZZIE: Mine does.

LAURA: Cut him some slack. He's been on his own for over ten years. It musta been lonely.

LIZZIE: I guess a wife can be replaced, but a mother . . . ? Never.

LAURA: Not ours, that's for sure.

LIZZIE: Hey! Nobody made a speech. Someone has to.

LAURA: Don't look at me.

LIZZIE: It's not a wedding without a toast to the bride. Hey, everyone!

LAURA: Oh / good god.

LIZZIE: Everyone, listen up! It's speech time!

LAURA: No, it's / not.

LIZZIE: Hey! Hey!

The music stops.

Friends, relatives, distinguished guests! My sister Laura and I wanna take this opportunity to welcome Marilyn to our small but mightily fucked-up family.

She looks at LAURA.

LAURA: Welcome! . . . Now, let's get / back to the—

LIZZIE: Marilyn, you've found a man who can love pretty much anyone or anything. I mean, heck, he managed to love my mom for more than eighteen years, and that could not have been easy, and, every once in a while, I get the feeling he might just love me, and that is definitely not easy.

LAURA: Lizzie—

LIZZIE: But I digress. Marilyn, you'll never be our real mom.

LAURA: Whoa.

LIZZIE: Because there's no substitute for the real thing. She was one of a kind. Our real mom was mangy and mean and wild as hell. She played rough and loved fiercely. Am I right, Laura?

LAURA: I don't think / this is—

LIZZIE: Am I right?!

LAURA: Sure. Yes, / you're—

LIZZIE: If—if she was here—

LAURA: Which she's not.

LIZZIE: But *if* she was, I know exactly what she'd do. She'd go feral. We're talkin' full coyote.

LAURA: Lizzie—

LIZZIE: She'd get down on her hands and knees—

LAURA: No.

LIZZIE: —take a deep breath all the way down to her hoodelee doodelee—

LAURA: Don't / do this.

LIZZIE: —point her snout up to the sky, and howl for all she was worth. / Like this:

LAURA prevents LIZZIE from getting down on her hands and knees.

LAURA: No, no, no! Stand up!

LIZZIE opens her mouth to howl just as LAURA covers it and stops the howl from happening.

No!

LIZZIE: *(through a covered mouth)* I'm trying to welcome Marilyn.

LAURA: Shhh. Please. Not like this. Fuck, I'll do it. Let me do it.

LIZZIE stops struggling. LAURA releases her.

LIZZIE: Speech!

LAURA: Marilyn, what Lizzie is trying to say is . . . our mom's a hard act to follow, but we can't imagine anyone being more suited to—to loving our dad than you. You make him happy and he deserves to be happy. You both do. Everyone deserves a shot at happiness. Isn't that right, Lizzie?

LIZZIE: What are you gonna do with all of Mom's / stuff?

LAURA: So, congratulations!

LIZZIE: A toast!

LAURA: To the bride!

LIZZIE: And my dad—the groom! Enough speechifying! Let's dance!

LAURA: Music!

The music starts up.

LIZZIE: Dance with me, Laura!

LAURA: Whatever you want, just behave yourself.

LIZZIE and LAURA dance.

LIZZIE: To the happy couple!

Happy, happy, happy!

LAURA: I said behave.

After some dancing, the music fades or changes to a slow dance. LIZZIE slow dances with LAURA.

LIZZIE: Laura? Are you happy?

LAURA: Occasionally.

LIZZIE: Me too. Sometimes I'm very, very happy and, other times, I'm not very happy at all.

LAURA: Take it easy on the booze, eh?

LIZZIE: I will. I need it tonight though so I can pretend to celebrate. They got a disco ball. I'm glad they did that. Reminds me of outer space. It's like a star exploded and we're smack dab in the middle of it.

LAURA: I'm exhausted. Let's go. David and I can give you a lift back to the hotel.

LIZZIE: Nah, I'm good. I got a few more dances in me. I'll walk.

LAURA: That'll take forever.

LIZZIE: Then I'll hitchhike.

LAURA: Don't be stupid.

LIZZIE: I got plenty of options. I bet the guy in the brown suit'll give me a ride if I ask nicely. He was giving me the eye earlier.

LAURA: He looks like a jackass.

LIZZIE: He does!

LIZZIE laughs.

God, I miss you. We gotta hang out more.

LAURA: Yeah, and you gotta drink less.

LIZZIE: That's for sure. One more year and I'll have my Bachelor of Science, but I have to get my marks up—way up—to be an astronaut.

LAURA: You were so brilliant. You still are.

LIZZIE: I'm gonna do it. *Obeshchayu*—that means I promise in Russian.

LAURA: See ya later, Valentina.

LIZZIE: *Da svidania*. Give my best to David.

LAURA: Get home safe.

LIZZIE turns back to the dance floor.

LIZZIE: Hey! You in the brown suit! Let's boogie, jackass!

A shift into the present.

LAURA: Get home safe.

Jesus, Lizzie! Why?

LIZZIE: . . .

LAURA: Huh? Why?

LIZZIE shrugs.

Cheek to cheek and breast to breast
Lock'd together in one nest

The past. LAURA and LIZZIE are at the police station.

(thirty years old) Lizzie! What the hell? This is crazy.

LIZZIE: *(thirty years old)* They aren't gonna press charges.

LAURA: Drunk and disorderly?

LIZZIE: The cops made it sound worse than it was.

LAURA: Assault?

LIZZIE: She started it.

LAURA: Oh my god.

LIZZIE: Well, she did. Chick spat in my hair.

LAURA: Jesus.

LIZZIE: I didn't wanna call you, but they insisted I get someone to pick me up.

LAURA: The cop said he found pills on you. Pills?

LIZZIE: Painkillers. I take 'em for the pain.

LAURA: You don't have any pain.

LIZZIE: Oh yes I do. I got the pain that comes from living day after day.

LAURA: You shouldn't mix booze with pills.

LIZZIE: I never took any.

LAURA: You just told me you did—for the pain.

LIZZIE: It was a joke. I never took a single one.

LAURA: But you have been drinking.

LIZZIE: Yes.

LAURA: Binging.

LIZZIE: You should apply for a job here. You'd make a great cop.

LAURA: I had no idea things were this bad.

LIZZIE: They aren't.

LAURA: That police officer is pretty familiar with you. How often are you here?

LIZZIE: This is the first time I've been in. I swear. I was just blowing off some steam. I've been studying hard. I'm under a lot of pressure. I gotta get my GPA higher so I can go to McGill or the U of A for my masters. There's still time. Roberta Bondar was forty-seven when she flew on the space shuttle *Discovery*. Deke Slayton was fifty-one on the Apollo–Soyuz Test Project. Valeri Polyakov, fifty-two. Dennis Tito, sixty . . . fuck . . . would you stop looking at me like that?

LAURA: Like what?

LIZZIE: Like, I don't know, like you're hurt or something, because I don't wanna hurt you.

LAURA: Of course you don't. I know that.

LIZZIE: . . . A few weeks ago, I saw a coyote crossing the Trans-Canada. Four lanes. Cars everywhere. A semi missed it by an inch and all I could do was watch.

LAURA: Did it make it?

LIZZIE: Yep. And guess what it did when it got to the other side?

LAURA: I dunno. Slunk into the bush?

LIZZIE: Nope. Turned right around and crossed the highway all over again, head down, dodging traffic the whole way back, like it was a game. Reminded me of Mom. I don't think it was a coincidence that it was a coyote I saw.

LAURA: Symbolic.

LIZZIE: Maybe I should try doing something else. Thousands of people wanna be astronauts. And there's what? A few chosen ones.

LAURA: But it's all you've ever wanted to do.

LIZZIE: The competition's fierce. Maybe it's too much for me.

LAURA: I don't understand. Why would you give up?

LIZZIE: I smell like Mom. She's coming out of every one of my pores. And I'm starting to sound like her too. She used to make all kinds of excuses. I don't wanna end up like her. I don't wanna be a coyote. I wanna be a better sister. I wanna be a better daughter. I wanna be someone, anyone. I wanna be a damn astronaut so bad.

LAURA: Then keep trying.

LIZZIE: But an astronaut cannot have a police record.

LAURA: You don't.

LIZZIE: Not yet.

LAURA: You won't.

LIZZIE: I have a problem, Laura!

LAURA: . . .

LIZZIE: I wanna get sober.

LAURA: I want that as much as you do.

LIZZIE: I can't do it on my own.

LAURA: I'll help you.

LIZZIE: No, I wanna go to rehab this time.

LAURA: Yeah, okay. I'm here for ya.

A shift into the present. LIZZIE*'s apartment.*

She suck'd and suck'd and suck'd the more
Fruits which that unknown orchard bore

If at first you don't succeed, try, try again.

LIZZIE: And again.

LAURA: And again and again and again.

The past. LAURA *and* LIZZIE *are at their father's funeral. A funeral hymn plays.*

(thirty-four years old) That was a whole lot of praying for a guy who wasn't religious.

LIZZIE: *(thirty-four years old)* Marilyn is. I wish they'd played Zeppelin or Floyd instead of all those hymns.

LAURA: "Stairway to Heaven." Dad woulda dug that.

LIZZIE: You know, there is one good thing about funerals.

LAURA: What's that?

LIZZIE: The egg salad sandwiches they serve in the hall afterwards. Those church ladies really know how to make 'em. I don't know how they do it.

LAURA: White bread, eggs, mayo, mustard, green onion, paprika. I'd make you one if you ever came to visit.

LIZZIE: I call you all the time.

LAURA: Not the same.

LIZZIE: I email you.

LAURA: I wanna see your face.

LIZZIE: You are right now.

LAURA: Not like this. I wanna see your face under different circumstances.

LIZZIE: I'm glad there wasn't an open casket.

LAURA: You think being cremated and divided by three is better?

LIZZIE: Than being six feet under? You bet I do. Darkness. Worms.

LAURA: Ugh.

LIZZIE: David didn't come.

LAURA: No, he didn't.

LIZZIE: I figured he'd be here.

LAURA: David left me.

LIZZIE: Oh shit.

LAURA: Yeah.

LIZZIE: I'm so sorry.

LAURA: Thanks. It breaks my heart.

LIZZIE: Of course it does. So, what are you gonna do?

LAURA: Sell the house. Move on. Never fall in love again.

LIZZIE: Oh, Laura.

LIZZIE hugs her.

Guess it's just you and me now.

LAURA: And Marilyn.

LIZZIE: She doesn't count.

LAURA: She's still family.

LIZZIE: Not if she can help it. Just you wait. We'll stop hearing from her. She'll fade away. Guaranteed.

LAURA: I thought I'd sprinkle my share of Dad's ashes on the farm beside the garage. He spent a lot of time out there. What are you gonna do with yours?

LIZZIE: Keep 'em. Gonna take Dad up in a rocket ship. Show him what the earth looks like from four hundred thousand kilometres away.

LAURA: Oh yeah? How are you gonna do that?

LIZZIE: I got into McGill. I start in the fall.

LAURA: Fuckin' aces, Lizard! I knew you could do it.

LIZZIE: Means I'll be moving to Montreal to do my masters.

LAURA: I'll come visit.

LIZZIE: All I had to do was get sober and stay that way. It's funny how much easier it is to study when you're not hungover or jonesin'.

LAURA: Good for you.

LIZZIE: Who knows? Maybe one day I'll be strapped into a seat aboard a rocket ship on the launch pad at the Space Center in Houston, feeling the rumble as the main engines ignite.

LAURA: Ten seconds to liftoff.

LIZZIE: Ten, nine, eight, seven, six, / five, four—

A shift into the present.

LAURA: Five, four, three, two, one—I don't understand. You had liftoff, Lizzie. You had nowhere to go but up. Up, up, up. Above the clouds. And beyond. You could've had it all, but then you had to go and fuck it up! Always!

The past. LAURA is driving. LIZZIE, very drunk, stumbles out in front of the car. The screech of brakes.

BOTH: *(thirty-six years old)* Aaaah!

LIZZIE doubles over laughing.

LAURA: Jesus!

LIZZIE crawls into the car.

LIZZIE: Incoming!

LAURA: Fuck, I nearly ran you over! You stepped right in front of the car. Don't do that!

LIZZIE: Pull it out and I'll suck it. Twenty bucks.

LAURA: What?!

LIZZIE: I'll suck it. Money up front.

LAURA: Lizzie!

LIZZIE: Yo. *(realizing)* Holy shit! Laura!

LAURA: Yeah. Remember me?

LIZZIE: You're Laura!

LAURA: What the hell are you doing out here?

LIZZIE: Duh. If you don't know that, you don't know dick! Ha! Dick!

LAURA: Oh my god.

LIZZIE: It's more about what they wanna do to me. Forwards, backwards, and sideways, baby!

LAURA: Oh my fucking god.

LIZZIE: Any way they want it.

LAURA: How long have you been doing this?

LIZZIE: Hitchhiking?

LAURA: No, sucking cock for twenty bucks.

LIZZIE: A girl's gotta do what a girl's gotta do.

LAURA: No, Lizzie, no, you don't have to do this.

LIZZIE: Maybe I like it.

LAURA: Please, don't say that! Jesus, this is so fucked. You never call me. And when I call, you don't answer. Then, when I go to your apartment, I find out you don't live there anymore—

LIZZIE: I got kicked out.

LAURA: —so I have to drive all over the city trying to find you.

LIZZIE: The lost is found!

LAURA: You're still lost.

LIZZIE: Ta da!

LAURA: You are so / so lost.

LIZZIE: Hey! Let's go on a road trip. A road trip heals all wounds.

LAURA: Lizzie.

LIZZIE: Let's drive. Keep me outta trouble. Drive!

LAURA: No. We're not going anywhere.

LIZZIE: Party pooper.

LAURA: You're completely wasted.

LIZZIE: Blatto.

LAURA: Again.

LIZZIE: Thud! Fell off the wagon. Try. Thud. Try. Thud. Try, try again. Thud.

LAURA sighs.

I know what you're thinking.

LAURA: Oh yeah?

LIZZIE: You think I feel sorry for myself. All you hear me saying is wah wah wah, boo fuckin' hoo.

LAURA: No, that's not / what I'm—

LIZZIE: *(overlapping)* Wah wah wah—

LAURA: That's not / what I'm—

LIZZIE: *(overlapping)* Boo fuckin' hoo. That's what you're thinking.

LAURA: I don't know what to think. Not anymore. I really don't.

LIZZIE: Wah wah wah, boo fuckin' hoo.

LAURA sighs, then grabs a bag from the back seat or from under LIZZIE's feet.

LAURA: Here. From the drive-through.

LIZZIE takes the bag.

LIZZIE: Yay!

She opens the wrapper.

A burg! Yeah! Cheese burg!

LAURA: Soak up some of that alcohol.

LIZZIE: Fries! Got anything to drink? Vodka?

LAURA: You've had enough.

LIZZIE eats. She's a mess—cheeseburger falling out of her mouth, so drunk she can barely chew.

Ugh. Chew with your mouth closed.

LIZZIE: This is good, Laura.

LAURA: I can't even look at you.

LIZZIE: This is really, really—

LAURA: Makes me sick.

LIZZIE: Really good. You're always takin' care of me.

LAURA: Cuz you can't take care of yourself.

LIZZIE: You're the best sister a girl could ask for.

LAURA: Sure.

LIZZIE: *"For there is no friend like a sister*
In calm or stormy weather"

Ha! That whole fuckin' poem is all up here.

LAURA: Good for you.

LIZZIE: Let's say it together.

"In calm or stormy / weather"

LAURA: Shut up and eat.

LIZZIE: Say it with me!

"To cheer one—"

LAURA: No.

LIZZIE: Say it!

LAURA: I don't remember it.

LIZZIE: Bullshit.

"To cheer one on the tedious—"

Come on, I know you know it.

LAURA: I don't.

LIZZIE: You do so.

"To cheer one—to cheer—"

Come on. You're fakin' like you forgot, ya fake.

LIZZIE stops eating.

Ugh. I can't eat any more.

LAURA: Then don't.

LIZZIE: Ugh. I don't—I don't feel so good. Ugh.

LAURA: In the bag. Do it in the bag!

LIZZIE throws up into the takeout bag.

LIZZIE: Ohhhh . . . Ohhhh.

LAURA: Fuck.

She hands LIZZIE a napkin.

Here.

LIZZIE: Ohhhhh.

LAURA: Clean yourself up.

LIZZIE: I'm sorry, Laura.

LAURA: Uh huh.

LIZZIE: I'm real, real, real sorry.

LAURA: Sure y'are.

LIZZIE: I am.

LAURA: As always.

LIZZIE: I drank waaay too much.

LAURA: You don't say.

LIZZIE: Oh man, I got wounds. You can't see 'em, but I got 'em.

LAURA: You think you're the only one?

LIZZIE: Mine are deep. I'm bleedin' out. I gotta drink to keep 'em from festering.

LAURA: No, you don't.

LIZZIE: I don't want 'em to get infected.

LAURA: Let me take you home.

LIZZIE: Home is where the heart is.

LAURA: Where you at these days?

LIZZIE: Here.

LAURA: On the street corner?

LIZZIE: Nearby. I can walk.

LAURA: I don't think you can.

LIZZIE: Watch this.

LIZZIE points at the pocket of her coat and casts a spell.

Ta zing!

She pulls out a mickey.

Ta da!

LAURA: Put that away.

LIZZIE: I gotta chase the burg down / with somethin'.

LAURA: Not in my car, you don't.

LIZZIE: Hey!

LAURA grabs the bottle.

LAURA: Give it here.

LIZZIE holds on to the bottle.

LIZZIE: No way.

LAURA: Lizzie!

LIZZIE pulls the bottle violently to her chest.

LIZZIE: No! It's mine!

LIZZIE drinks.

Hair of the dog!

LIZZIE barks.

LAURA: You're disgusting.

LIZZIE: Cheers, big ears!

LIZZIE drinks.

LAURA: How can you do this to yourself?

LIZZIE: . . .

LAURA: How can you do this to me?

LIZZIE: . . .

LAURA: How?

LIZZIE: Like mother, like daughter.

LAURA: You're not anything like her.

LIZZIE: I'm even more of a fuck-up than she was.

LAURA: You don't have to be.

LIZZIE points at herself.

LIZZIE: Fuck-up, failure, bottom-feeder.

LIZZIE drinks.

LAURA: You had so much potential.

LIZZIE: I'm fuckin' strong. Feel my muscle.

LAURA: You could've been good at so many things.

LIZZIE: Astrophysics!

LAURA: You could have.

LIZZIE: Hey! I know! I could work in the gift shop at the Space Science Center.

LAURA: You gotta stop.

LIZZIE: That'll be five fixty-seven please.

LIZZIE drinks.

LAURA: Lizzie, you gotta stop—for good.

LIZZIE: When I finish this, I'm done.

LAURA: You don't have to finish it.

LIZZIE: Never ever leave a bottle unfinished. That's a / rule.

LIZZIE drinks.

LAURA: You could stop right now if you wanted to.

LIZZIE: Easy for you to say.

LAURA: You've done it before.

LIZZIE: It always ends the same way—with me startin' right back up again.

LAURA grabs the bottle again.

LAURA: Stop.

LIZZIE: I can't.

LAURA: Stop.

LIZZIE: I wanna finish it.

LAURA: Stop, stop, stop, stop, stop!

She gets the bottle away from LIZZIE.

LIZZIE *screams.*

That's enough.

LIZZIE: Give it back.

LAURA: No.

LIZZIE: Give it!

LAURA: Nope.

LIZZIE: Pleeease.

LAURA: . . .

LIZZIE *whimpers, coyote-like.*

. . .

LIZZIE: Coyote needs a drink.

LAURA: You're not a coyote, Lizzie. You're a human being.

LIZZIE: I wanna be human again.

LAURA: Start acting like one.

LIZZIE: I wanna be human again. I wanna be human again. I wanna be human again. / I wanna be human again.

LAURA: Start acting like a human being and not some fucking crazed animal!

LIZZIE: Human!

LAURA: . . .

LIZZIE: Mom told me why coyotes howl, but she never told me why humans do. Why do *you* think humans howl?

LAURA: All kinds of reasons.

LIZZIE: Name one.

LAURA: Seriously?

LIZZIE: I wanna hear you name one reason. One!

LAURA: Heartbreak.

LIZZIE: Yeah. Another.

LAURA: Loneliness.

LIZZIE: And another.

LAURA: Sorrow.

LIZZIE: And one more.

LAURA: That's all I got.

LIZZIE: Come on, one more! One more one more one more one more one—

LAURA: Rage.

LIZZIE: Yeah! Rage! Yeah, rage rage rage rage rage / rage

LAURA: They are full of rage! Because their sister's a drunk and they can't get her to quit no matter how hard they try so they have to stand by helplessly watching as she destroys herself repeatedly and this makes them want to scream and punch things and tear their hair out by the roots and—and strangle the whole fuckin' world!

LIZZIE: Sounds like a good reason to howl.

LAURA: Is it ever.

LIZZIE: Go ahead. Howl.

LAURA: No, thanks.

LIZZIE: Come on.

LAURA: No.

LIZZIE: Why not?

LAURA: Because if I start— It's not my style.

LIZZIE: Chickenshit.

LAURA pours out the bottle.

No! No!

LAURA lets the empty bottle fall to the ground.

Bitch!

LAURA: I don't know how to help you.

LIZZIE: Don't bother. Drive / away.

LAURA: I don't know how.

LIZZIE: It's easy. When I get out, you put the car in drive, / put your foot on the gas—

LAURA: No, I don't know how.

LIZZIE: —and get as far away from me as you / possibly can!

LAURA: I don't know how to help you anymore, Lizzie! Tell me how I can help you.

LIZZIE: You can't. There's nothing more you can do. Nothing! I'm beyond help.

LAURA: Then you've gotta find a way to look after yourself.

LIZZIE: No problem.

LAURA: Or if you're determined to self-destruct, don't force me to watch. You're on your own. I'm taking care of myself for a change.

LIZZIE: Okey-dokey.

LAURA: Don't make me do this . . . please.

LIZZIE: Don't touch me.

LAURA: Please, / Lizzie.

LIZZIE: Hands off!

LAURA: I don't wanna / do this.

LIZZIE: I want out. Lemme / out!

LAURA: Lizard, please. I need / you. I—

LIZZIE: I want out! Now! / Now!

LAURA: OKAY! GET OUT!

LIZZIE: / I AM!

LAURA: GET THE FUCK OUT OF MY CAR! BETTER YET, GET THE FUCK OUT OF MY LIFE! I'M DONE WITH ALL OF YOUR BULLSHIT! DONE! I AM SO DONE, SO SO SO FUCKING DONE WITH ALL OF IT, WITH EVERYTHING, EVERY LAST FUCKING THING!

LIZZIE: . . .

LAURA: You are wrecking me.

LIZZIE: You think I don't know that?

LAURA: I can't take this. It hurts way too much.

LIZZIE: No shit.

LAURA: I cannot be your sis . . .

LIZZIE: Say it.

LAURA: I cannot be your sister anymore.

LIZZIE: Attagirl.

LAURA howls—a wild, tortured release. The howl brings her back to the present and she finds herself, once again, in LIZZIE's apartment.

LAURA: And then . . . then I drove away. At the end of the block I turned left and you disappeared from sight. Two days went by and I didn't hear from you. No surprise. I couldn't pick up the phone either.

This morning, my doorbell rang. It was two police officers. They introduced themselves—Officer Wilson and I can't for the life of me remember the other one's name. She asked if she and her partner could come in, suggested I have a seat, and then told me your body had been found in an apartment downtown. She asked if you struggled with addiction and I told her you were an alcoholic, that you'd been one for years. She nodded and said that you'd—you'd asphyxiated on your . . . they thought maybe you'd been trying to quit and that you'd gone into severe withdrawal. She said I could request a further autopsy. I declined. I got the address to where you'd been found and came here. The building manager gave me the key and I let myself in. The room was . . . it was . . . a lot. And on the bed, beside the pillow, I found the book of poems.

She picks up the book of poems.

I read the inscription.

(reads) "To Laura and Lizzie,"

BOTH: "Always look after each other. Love, Mom."

LIZZIE: You couldn't save me.

LAURA: I tried.

LIZZIE: In "Goblin Market" one sister saves the other, so why couldn't you save me?

LAURA: Because life isn't a poem.

LIZZIE: No?

LAURA: It just isn't.

LIZZIE: . . .

LAURA: Get into bed and pull the blankets tight.

LIZZIE: . . .

LAURA: Get in! Quick!

They climb into bed. As they do, the stars from the girl-made tin-can solar system fill the room.

LIZZIE: The girl-made tin-can solar system.

LAURA: That's the North Star—

LIZZIE: —the brightest—

LAURA: —it leads you to the Little Dipper. The Little Dipper pours into Ursa Major, the Big Bear, then, across to Gemini—the twins.

LIZZIE: You remember.

LAURA: It's all I can do now.

LAURA presses the book of poems to her chest.

Laura and Lizzie.

We are two little twin girl fetuses. Our hearts beating. Whooshwhoosh. I reach out for your hand. I reach and reach . . .

LAURA howls softly. It is reminiscent of the howl LIZZIE made in the car after their mother died. By the time LAURA's howl has ended, LIZZIE has faded into the shadows, leaving LAURA alone in the silence.

End of play.

ACKNOWLEDGEMENTS

I would like to thank Workshop West Playwrights' Theatre, Vern Thiessen, the Citadel Theatre Playwrights Lab, Colleen Murphy, Brian Dooley, Daryl Cloran, Nadien Chu, Miranda Allen, Patricia Darbasie, Lora Brovold, Ian Arnold, Tarragon Theatre, Andrea Romaldi, Esther Jun, Richard Rose, Tamara Podemski, Sarah Podemski, Patrick Fraser, Oscar, and of course Christina Rossetti for writing her incredible poem, "Goblin Market," which provided me with much inspiration.

Beth Graham is a playwright and an actor. She was born in Antigonish, Nova Scotia, grew up in Cochrane, Alberta, and now lives in Edmonton. She was a finalist for the Governor General's Literary Award for Drama in 2015 for her play *The Gravitational Pull of Bernice Trimble*. She co-wrote *The Drowning Girls* with Daniela Vlaskalic and Charlie Tomlinson. Beth is a graduate of the University of Alberta's BFA acting program, where she is currently the Lee Playwright in Residence.

First edition: November 2020
Printed and bound in Canada by Rapido Books, Montreal

Jacket illustration by Myriam Wares
Author photo © David Spowart

PLAYWRIGHTS CANADA PRESS
202-269 Richmond St. w.
Toronto, ON
M5V 1X1

416.703.0013
info@playwrightscanada.com
www.playwrightscanada.com
@playcanpress